MW00877443

The Serpent Seed: Debunked

Minister Dante Fortson

The Serpent Seed: Debunked

Copyright © 2010 by Minister Dante Fortson

Website: www.MinisterFortson.com

ISBN 10: 1453849661
ISBN 13: 9781453849668

All scripture quotations in this book are taken from the King James Version of the Bible except where noted. Words appearing in bold are the author's own emphasis.

First Edition

www.ImpactAgendaMedia.com

This book is dedicated to everyone that has
ever been deceived by a false doctrine.

www.MinisterFortson.com

Table of Contents

Introduction

Recently, I've become heavily involved in debating the Serpent Seed Theory, and in my opinion, when we use the Bible as our basis, there is not much to debate at all. The Bible is 100% clear as to the origin of Cain. When we use outside sources that are in contradiction to the Bible, this clarity is removed.

All points in this book will be made using only the Bible and a Strong's Concordance. While certain English words may allow for the twisting of scripture, the Hebrew and Greek words are very precise and twisting them is not as easy.

> "For the time will come when they will not endure sound doctrine; but after their own lusts shall they heap to themselves teachers, having itching ears; And they shall turn away their ears from the truth, and shall be turned unto fables." - 2 Timothy 2:3-4

In His service,

Minister Dante Fortson

Minister Dante Fortson

Chapter 1: The Eden Scenario

The origin of the Serpent Seed Theory begins in Eden and is based on very inaccurate assumptions made by outside texts. Because the Bible is the basis for what we as Christians believe, we will only be using the Bible to explore whether or not this theory has any validity. One sure sign of a false doctrine, is one that cannot use the Bible as its foundation. After you finish this book, you are encouraged to buy a copy for everyone you know. So what exactly is Serpent Seed Theory?

What Is The Serpent Seed Theory?

Serpent Seed Theory teaches that God gave Adam and Eve permission to eat from every tree in the garden except one. That tree was the tree of the knowledge of good and evil, which was not actually a tree. The theory teaches that eating from the tree actually represents sex with the serpent, and once Adam and Eve ate, their eyes were opened. God then told the serpent that He would put conflict between the serpent's seed and the seed of the woman. The seed of the serpent is believed to be Cain and the seed of the woman is believed to be Abel. All non-whites are usually attributed as coming from Cain, and thus descended from the devil, while all whites come from Abel, and are thus God's chosen people. This is a very interesting story that entices those with "itching ears", but what really happened in the garden?

What Really Happened In The Garden?

According to Serpent Seed Theory, Eve was seduced by the serpent into having sex with him. She then convinces Adam to do the same, and that is why they were ashamed to be naked, but does the Bible support this theory?

> "Now the serpent was more subtil than any beast of the field which the LORD God had made. And he said unto the woman, Yea, hath God said, Ye shall not eat of every tree of the garden? And the woman said unto the serpent, We may eat of the fruit of the trees of the garden: But of the fruit of the

tree which is in the midst of the garden, God hath said, Ye shall not eat of it, neither shall ye touch it, lest ye die. And the serpent said unto the woman, Ye shall not surely die: For God doth know that in the day ye eat thereof, then your eyes shall be opened, and ye shall be as gods, knowing good and evil. And when the woman saw that the tree was good for food, and that it was pleasant to the eyes, and a tree to be desired to make one wise, she took of the fruit thereof, and did eat, and gave also unto her husband with her; and he did eat." - Genesis 3:1-6

Before we examine this passage, it is important to point out that the Serpent Seed Theory applies the following interpretation to the objects in the story:

- Adam - a literal man.
- Eve - a literal woman.
- Serpent - a literal angel named Lucifer.
- The Tree of Knowledge - figuratively represents the serpent.
- Fruit - sex.

Now that we know how those that hold the view interpret the passage, we can take a look at how the Bible defends itself against such ridiculous ideas. Adam, Eve, and the serpent are all literal in the passage, so it is more important to figure out how the Bible portrays the tree and the fruit. Here are the main Hebrew words we will look at for this part of the text:

- Tree - ets (pine, plank, wood, stick, timber, tree)
- Fruit - peri (fruit, foliage)
- Eat - akal (eat, devour, consume)

In the context of the passage there is nothing about the tree that indicates it is figurative and not literal. They literally consumed fruit from a tree. Furthermore, there is already a serpent in the garden, so there would be no need to also have a tree that represents the same creature. Also, if we apply the law of interpretation, every other tree in the garden would have to represent sex with something. In Genesis 2:16 God tells them that they can eat from every tree in the garden except one. Was God saying that Adam and Eve could have sex with

2

everything in the garden except Satan? The more questions we ask, the clearer the absurdity of this theory becomes.

The next problem occurs once Adam and Eve are kicked out of the Garden. God places cherubim at the east of Eden to protect the way of the Tree of Life. If we apply Serpent Seed interpretation across the board, it would imply that God was using His highest ranking angels to stop Adam and Eve from having sex with a "tree" that they previously were allowed to have sex with. Traditionally, the Tree of Life has been interpreted as a literal tree that points to the redemption of Christ. When referencing the tree of knowledge, those that hold to the Serpent Seed Theory, interpret it as figurative, but change the tree of life to literal in order to avoid teaching that the tree represented sex with God. A huge red flag that someone is twisting scripture is when they start to apply different interpretations to the same types of objects in the same passage (one literal and one figurative).

   ✓   Debunked: Tree represents the serpent.
   ✓   Debunked: Fruit represents sex with the serpent.
   ✓   Debunked: Eating refers to partaking in the sexual act.

When questioned about the above interpretation, Serpent Seed Theorists will rarely, if ever use the Bible to explain how they reached their conclusions. After failing to make the above point, it is argued that there was something special about the fruit that made them ashamed to be naked, so let's look at the verse first.

> "And the eyes of them both were opened, and they knew that they were naked; and they sewed fig leaves together, and made themselves aprons." - Genesis 3:7

The Bible itself seems straight forward that their eyes were opened and they suddenly realized they were naked. According to those that hold the Serpent Seed Theory, it was sex with the serpent that opened their eyes, but there is nothing in the Hebrew or English that would indicate that sex took place. Here are a few Hebrew words to consider:

- Eyes – ayin (eye)
- Opened - paqach – (to open the senses)
- Knew – yada (know, knew, acknowledge)
- Naked – erom (naked)

Now we see that their senses were opened after eating this fruit. Neither the Hebrew nor English indicate that they became sexually aware. It is only assumed by Serpent Seed Theorists, that they were sexually unaware. It is very interesting to note that the word *yada* is the same word used to refer to sex in the Bible, but take note that this act of knowing refers to their nakedness. Even if we interpret this "knowing" as having sex, it is only used to refer to Adam and Eve's nakedness. There is no mention of "knowing" the tree or the serpent. The most likely interpretation is that they "acknowledged their own nakedness", thus explaining why they sewed fig leaves together to cover themselves.

Another problem we encounter is the false belief that Adam and Eve did not know about sex before eating from this tree. If we read the Bible carefully, we find that having sex was God's first commandment to them.

"And God blessed them, and God said unto them, Be fruitful, and multiply, and replenish the earth, and subdue it: and have dominion over the fish of the sea, and over the fowl of the air, and over every living thing that moveth upon the earth." – Genesis 1:28

We see that the very first chapter in the Bible contains the command to be like fruit and multiply. Have you ever met a person that can multiply themselves without having sex? Based on that single verse, we can debunk the belief that Adam and Eve were not aware of sex.

✓ Debunked: Adam and Eve were not sexually aware.

4

The Seduction of Adam and Eve

According to Serpent Seed Theorists, Eve was "wholly seduced" by the serpent which includes sexually. According to the theory, after Eve ate the fruit, she then brought the fruit to Adam and he ate. If we follow their line of interpretation, this means that Adam also had sex with the serpent. Since both Lucifer and Adam are depicted as male, the Serpent Seed Theory is in fact stating that both Adam and Lucifer are homosexuals. You will not generally hear Serpent Seed Theorists come right out and say Adam was a homosexual. The tactic is to lure people in with the story of Eve having sex while avoiding the mention of homosexuality. This will become very important as we progress through this book.

This business of sex in the garden is based on the Hebrew word "beguiled", so let's take a look at the verse and then at the Hebrew word translated as beguiled.

"And the LORD God said unto the woman, What is this that thou hast done? And the woman said, The serpent beguiled me, and I did eat." - Genesis 3:13

- Beguiled - nasha (lead astray, beguiled, deceive, morally deceive)

As we can see, nothing in the Bible or in the Hebrew translation of the word beguile implies that Eve had sex with the serpent. This brings us back to addressing the belief that Adam had a homosexual encounter. When we get to the New Testament, we find an interesting verse.

"And Adam was not deceived, but the woman being deceived was in the transgression." - 1 Timothy 2:4

If we take the above verse at face value, we see that Adam was not deceived, which means he knew what he was doing. If that is true, it means that Adam knowingly participated in a homosexual act with Lucifer. There is one huge problem with that theory. If the theory is true, it means God created both

5

Lucifer and Adam as homosexuals or possibly even bi-sexuals. This provides ammunition for the argument that homosexuality is not a choice, but part of the intended genetic makeup of a person. If God had created Adam as a homosexual, He would have also made a man for Adam to be with and not just a woman when Adam longed for a mate. Based on what we know from the Bible we can conclude that this part of the Serpent Seed Theory is false.

✓ Debunked: Eve had sex with the serpent.
✓ Debunked: Adam had sex with the serpent.

Giving Birth In The Flesh

One argument made by those that hold to the Serpent Seed Theory is that because Eve at the fruit, she would now have to give birth in the flesh. Here is the specific verse that announces Eve's curse.

> "Unto the woman he said, I will greatly multiply thy sorrow and thy conception; in sorrow thou shalt bring forth children; and thy desire shall be to thy husband, and he shall rule over thee." - Genesis 3:16

The first thing we should notice is that the Bible does not mention that Eve would be cursed to give birth in the flesh. It clearly states that she would give birth in sorrow. Because this verse does not support Serpent Seed theory, one tactic is to reinterpret the word based on Targums or outside sources instead of using the Strong's Concordance. Let's look at what the Hebrew says:

- 1st Sorrow - itstsabon (pain, effort)
- 2nd Sorrow - esteb (physical pain, suffering, painful toil)
- Conception - heron (childbirth, conception)

The word sorrow appears twice, but there are two different words used, neither of which refers to Eve suddenly turning into flesh from eating either a real or figurative fruit. There is

6

also another huge hurdle that must be leaped if we are to accept that Eve turned to flesh.

> "And Adam said, This is now bone of my bones, and flesh of my flesh: she shall be called Woman, because she was taken out of Man." - Genesis 2:23

As we can clearly read, Adam refers to himself and Eve as flesh in Genesis 2. Why would he refer to them as flesh if they previously were not flesh?

✓ Debunked: Eve turned to flesh after eating the fruit.

The Prophecy of Two Seeds

According to those that hold to the Serpent Seed Theory, the prophecy of strife between the two seeds refers to Cain and Abel. Before we debunk this false interpretation, let's look at what the verse says.

> "And I will put enmity between thee and the woman, and between thy seed and her seed; it shall bruise thy head, and thou shalt bruise his heel." - Genesis 3:15

Both sides of the debate accept that the prophecy of the two seeds refers to two different literal offspring. However, there is something very strange about the prophecy because it refers to the "seed of the woman" or "her seed". The first and most important thing to note is that it is grammatically and biologically incorrect to refer to a woman as having the seed. In every culture on earth, the seed comes from the man. This is clearly a prophecy of the virgin birth, and not predictive of the conflict between Cain and Abel. Furthermore, neither Cain nor Abel was born of a virgin, as we will see in the next chapter.

The last part of the prophecy predicts that the seed of the woman would crush the head of the serpent's seed. However, when we read the story of Cain and Abel, it is the supposed son of the serpent (Cain) that manages to kill or crush the head of the supposed seed of the woman (Abel). The entire scenario is

opposite of the prophecy, which shows that God was not referring to the future births of Cain and Abel.

✓ Debunked: The two seeds were Cain and Abel.

Hidden Serpent Seed Teachings

❖ God created Adam with homosexual desires.
❖ Adam was either homosexual or bi-sexual.

Debunked In This Chapter

✓ Debunked: Tree represents the serpent.
✓ Debunked: Fruit represents sex with the serpent.
✓ Debunked: Eating refers to partaking in the sexual act.
✓ Debunked: Tree Represents Sex
✓ Debunked: Eve had sex with the serpent.
✓ Debunked: Adam had sex with the serpent.
✓ Debunked: Adam and Ever were not sexually aware.
✓ Debunked: Eve turned to flesh after eating the fruit.
✓ Debunked: The two seeds were Cain and Abel.

Chapter 2: The Birth of Cain

According to Serpent Seed Theory, Cain was conceived inside of the garden, but according to the Bible, both Cain and Abel were only conceived after the couple was outside of the Garden. Even after completely ignoring what the Bible has to say, Serpent Seed Theorists attempt to make the argument that Cain was still the son of the serpent, but let's look at what the Bible says.

"And Adam knew Eve his wife; and she conceived, and bare Cain, and said, I have gotten a man from the LORD. And she again bare his brother Abel. And Abel was a keeper of sheep, but Cain was a tiller of the ground." - Genesis 4:1-2

The English is pretty straight forward. Notice how a big deal is made about Cain, but Abel is merely a footnote in the story. In my honest opinion, God saw the rise of this false theory and prepared for it in advance. Let's look at a few of the Hebrew words in this passage:

- Conceived - harah (came to be with child, became preganant)
- Bare - yalad (bear, give birth, become the father, bring forth)
- Said - amar (declared, boasted, said)
- Man - ish (man)
- Lord - YHVH

The order of events and the meaning of the words prove that Adam is indeed the father of Cain, according to the Bible. Serpent Seed Theorists will always avoid getting into the Hebrew meanings of most verses and will always find some way to twist it to fit their view. Something important to take note of is that the word "yalad" also means to become a father, which refers to the only male recorded as having sex with Eve, and that would be Adam.

If Cain was the son of the serpent, there would be no reason for Eve to boast that she had received a man from the Lord. The second problem is that Cain is referred to as *ish*, which is not the term used to refer to the hybrid offspring. There are two terms used in reference to hybrids and those words are

Nephilim and sometimes *gibborim*. Since Cain is called a man and he is referred to as fully human, it is only logical to conclude that Cain was fully human and fully the son of Adam.

✓ Debunked: Adam was not Cain's father.

The Genealogy of Adam, Cain, and Seth

Around this area of Serpent Seed Theory is where it gets a little confusing. Some say that Adam does not appear in Cain's genealogy, and some say that Cain does not appear in Adam's genealogy. That teaching is completely false, no matter how we look at it. All of Genesis 4 focuses on Cain and includes a genealogy. We have already seen that Genesis 4:1 starts off by going out of its way to point out that Eve did not get pregnant by Adam until they were outside of the garden, and Cain was definitely fully human. The point that Serpent Seed Theorists try to make is that Adam does not appear at the head of Cain's genealogy in Genesis 4:17-22. When we take an honest look at the Bible we find the same method of recording genealogies all throughout the text. In Genesis 10, when we examine the genealogies of Shem, Ham, and Japheth. Noah is only mentioned once in the chapter as being the father of all three. There is nothing strange about recording the genealogy in this manner.

✓ Debunked: Adam is not included in Cain's genealogy.

The next argument that is used comes from Genesis 5 and the genealogy contained therein. Serpent Seed Theorists incorrectly point out that the genealogy always comes through the oldest son, but this particular genealogy only focuses on the line of Seth. There would be no reason for Cain's name to appear in Seth's genealogy. The second and most important point is that many genealogies appear in the Bible in which the youngest son is used for God's purpose and not the oldest son.

- Seth - Youngest son of Adam and Eve
- Shem - Youngest son of Noah
- Isaac - Youngest son of Abraham and Sarah
- Jacob - Youngest son of Isaac and Rebecca
- Judah - Youngest son of Jacob and Leah
- Benjamin - Youngest son of Jacob and Rachel

If we look at Saul, the first king of Israel, he is chosen from the tribe of Benjamin. Benjamin was the youngest son of Jacob and Rachel. When he is replaced as king, God chooses David from the line of Judah. Although Judah was not Jacob's youngest son in general, he was the youngest son of Leah, his first wife. The line of Judah is the line through which Christ would eventually come. We can clearly see from Biblical examples that the oldest son is not always the chosen son.

✓ Debunked: Cain does not appear in Adam's genealogy.

When we look at the Bible as a whole, we can see that man's reasoning is easily proven wrong by the wisdom of God. The oldest son is not always the son through which the promise comes.

How Do We Learn To Sin?

One argument that Serpent Seed Theorists use as evidence for Lucifer being the father of Cain is the sin that he committed. They claim that someone had to teach Cain how to sin. The following verse is usually used to support that view.

> "Ye are of your father the devil, and the lusts of your father ye will do. **He was a murderer from the beginning**, and abode not in the truth, because there is no truth in him. When he speaketh a lie, he speaketh of his own: for he is a liar, and the father of it." - John 8:44

This verse will come up again later on in this book, but for now we are just going to look at the statement, "he was a

11

murderer from the beginning". Serpent Seed Theorists tie this statement to Cain killing Abel. However, the birth of Cain and Abel is not the beginning. The beginning occurs in Genesis 1:1 and it gets even further away if we consider the possibility of the Gap Theory.

Jesus' reference to Lucifer being a murderer from the beginning seems to have other implications that are reflected in the book of Ezekiel.

"By the multitude of thy merchandise **they have filled the midst of thee with violence**, and thou hast sinned: therefore I will cast thee as profane out of the mountain of God: and I will destroy thee, O covering cherub, from the midst of the stones of fire." - Ezekiel 28:16

This reference in Ezekiel is usually interpreted as referring to Lucifer as the covering cherub. The most likely scenario is that these statements are referring to events surrounding the fall of Lucifer from heaven. The fall of Lucifer is one of the biggest events in the Bible, but unfortunately there is very little information on the subject. When we step back and look at the big picture, we see that it is highly unlikely that either Ezekiel or Jesus was associating Lucifer with Cain.

As humans we are born into sin and have no need for someone to teach us how to commit specific sins. Cain could have learned how to kill Abel based on the killing of animals for the sacrifice. There are others that believe that the knowledge of killing was passed on genetically through Lucifer. If we accept this interpretation, we also have to consider that homosexuality was passed down genetically through Adam, according to Serpent Seed Theory. When we consider the implications of this belief, it eliminates the demonizing of one lineage over the other, and as a result, Serpent Seed Theorists will avoid talking about Adam potentially passing on homosexual genes.

12

We do not know exactly how Cain killed Abel, but we do know that it was this sin that was punished by God. Some believe God punished this sin by leaving a mark on Cain. Let's take a look at the text and see what the mark was really about.

The Mark of Cain

The mark of Cain has been debated for a very long time. Was it a blessing or was it a curse? If we rely on the Bible to tell us what the mark of Cain was, we can put the debate to rest once and for all.

> "Behold, thou hast driven me out this day from the face of the earth; and from thy face shall I be hid; and I shall be a fugitive and a vagabond in the earth; and it shall come to pass, that every one that findeth me shall slay me. And the LORD said unto him, Therefore whosoever slayeth Cain, vengeance shall be taken on him sevenfold. And the LORD set a mark upon Cain, lest any finding him should kill him." - Genesis 4:14-15

There are some that do not believe that Cain repented for his wrong doing. However, custom usually dictates what is considered repentance. Throughout the Bible we see repentance represented by sitting in ashes, pouring ashes on the head, or the tearing of clothes. In some cultures, public humiliation is considered an act of repentance. In this same regard, we see Cain begging for mercy because his punishment is too much for him to bear.

We can clearly read that the mark is not placed on Cain until after he pleads with God about his punishment being too much to bear. Because of this murder, God was going to hide His face from him, he was going to be a fugitive, and he was going to be homeless. This mark becomes an example of God's grace and mercy, even after commission of a sinful act.

13

Even when we look at these facts, Serpent Seed Theorists will disregard the Biblical text in favor of outside sources, in an attempt to turn the mark of Cain into a punishment.

"And the LORD said unto him, Therefore whosoever slayeth Cain, vengeance shall be taken on him sevenfold. And the LORD set a mark upon Cain, lest any finding him should kill him." - Genesis 4:15

Here are a few words in Hebrew that give us insight into what was really going on with the mark:

- Slayeth - harag (kill, murder, put to death)
- Vengeance - naqam (revenge, punishment)
- Mark - owth (mark, miracle, sign, token)

We can clearly see that from both the Hebrew and the English, this mark was given as a form of protection and there is nothing bad associated with the mark. The Bible does not say that the mark was a curse and the Bible does not say that the mark was dark skin. These are lies concocted by Serpent Seed Theorists in order to demonize Cain and ethnic races. As we examine the rest of the Bible, there are two more examples that show God reserves His mark only for people that He does not want harm to come to.

- Those with the mark were spared from death (Ezekiel 9:6).
- 144,000 spared from the wrath to come (Revelation 7:1-8).

Based on the context of the Cain story and the other two places where the mark of God appears, it is logical to conclude that God does not place His mark on people He hates, but to protect the people that He loves.

✓ Debunked: The mark of Cain was a curse.

When Was Abel Killed?

There are some that believe that Cain and Abel lived until about 1,000 years before the flood. While it is entirely possible that Cain lived that long, it is nothing more than speculation. According to the Bible, Abel definitely died long before then. If we plot a timeline, we know that Noah's flood occurs 1,656 years after Adam's creation. According to the Bible:

> "And Adam knew his wife again; and she bare a son, and called his name Seth: For God, said she, hath appointed me another seed instead of Abel, whom Cain slew." - Genesis 4:25

We read that Seth was given to Eve to replace Abel, but how old was Abel when he was murdered? According to Genesis 5:3, Seth was born when Adam was 130 years old. So if we make the assumption that Seth was born the same year, the oldest Abel could have been when he died was 130 years old.

✓ Debunked: Abel was older than 130 when he died.

Did Lamech Kill Cain?

Part of the Serpent Seed Theory states that Cain's descendant Lamech is the one that eventually kills him. If we read through Genesis 4, we will see that the name of the man Lamech kills is never mentioned. Finally, there is a verse that lets us know that Lamech did not actually kill Cain.

> "And Lamech said unto his wives, Adah and Zillah, Hear my voice; ye wives of Lamech, hearken unto my speech: for I have slain a man to my wounding, and a young man to my hurt. If Cain shall be avenged sevenfold, truly Lamech seventy and sevenfold. " - Genesis 4:23-24

God promised to take vengeance on whoever killed Cain, yet we see that Lamech is expecting to be avenged seventy seven fold. Why would he be expecting protection from God if he had just killed a man that God promised to avenge? Lamech would have fallen under God's vengeance as promised to Cain, if any man killed him. It is likely that Lamech thought of himself as somewhat righteous because he expected to be avenged seventy seven fold. It is also very likely that the person he killed was not Cain. The underlying teaching to this theory is that if Lamech actually killed Cain, God did not keep His promise, thus making Him a liar.

✓ Debunked: Lamech killed Cain.

Was Seth's Entire Line Righteous?

As part of this twisted theory, there are many that claim that Seth's entire line was righteous and Cain's entire line was unrighteous. This stretch is made in order to give weight to their twisted theory. According to the Bible, God gave Seth to Adam and Eve as a replacement for the murdered Abel. However, there are several things that indicate that the entire line was by no means righteous.

The sons of Seth may have been godly, but there is no indication in the scripture that they are called the sons of God nor is there any indication that they were all godly. Genesis Chapter 6 makes absolutely no references to Cain or Seth in the Hebrew, Greek, Latin, or English translations. In order to make this theory to fit, those that hold this view need to make their own changes to words in the actual Biblical text. Cain killed Abel, so it is assumed that his entire line is ungodly, but God forgave Cain and placed a mark of protection on him. The theory also runs into two more Biblical problems when we get to Luke and John.

> "Which was the son of Enos, which was the son of Seth, which was the son of Adam, which was the son of God." - Luke 3:38

Luke is tracing the bloodline of the Messiah back until he reaches God. Notice that Luke refers to Seth as "the son of Adam" and then to Adam as the son of God. In Hebrew, Adam means "man", so Luke is calling Seth the son of a man. This does not seem to be coincidental in the least bit. Before the resurrection of Christ, the only two men referred to as sons of God, by name, were Adam and Jesus. John testifies to this also.

> "But as many as received him, to them gave he power to become the sons of God, even to them that believe on his name:" - John 1:12

There are only two ways to become a son of God. One way is by being a direct creation of God, and the other way is receiving Christ. If Seth was not a direct creation by God and Christ had not yet been resurrected, how did Seth's line come to be called the sons of God? Something else that is worthy of pointing out is that if the phrase referred to the sons of Seth, it means that they initiated the disobedience to God, not Cain's line. The scripture indicates that the sons of God took wives of all that "they chose". There are also two more questions that arise from this theory:

1. Why did Seth's entire lineage except for Noah's family die in the flood?
2. Why were they in the company of Satan in Job Chapters 1 and 2?

We can clearly see that the evidence so far argues against the sons of God actually being the sons of Seth. Another major stumbling block for the theory is lack of scriptural support. Seth may have been the replacement for Abel's death, but nowhere does it say that his entire line was godly. Another verse that adds a nail to this coffin is found in Hebrews:

> "For verily he took not on him the nature of angels; but he took on him the seed of Abraham." - Hebrews 2:16

Here the Bible refers to the seed of Abraham, but we do not assume that the Bible really means someone other than Abraham, so why make the same assumption about Genesis Chapter 6? We know the Bible is talking about the Nation of Israel specifically. Why do some try to change the Word of God to fit their own personal beliefs? The Bible says what it means and means what it says. When it refers to the sons of Elohim (God), it is not referring to anyone other than God. When it says daughters of Adam, it is not referring to anyone other than Adam. When it says Abraham, it is not referring to anyone other than Abraham.

God's Word	Man's Word
Sons of God	Sons of Seth
Daughters of Adam	Daughters of Cain

"Add thou not unto his words, lest he reprove thee, and thou be found a liar." - Proverbs 30:6

Genealogy of Seth

Seth is the son that God blessed Adam and Eve with after Cain killed Abel. There is no scriptural reference to Seth's line being godly, but it seems to be an invention of man to twist the scripture to fit their beliefs instead of twisting their beliefs to fit scripture. Let's take a look at Seth's line starting with Adam and concluding with Noah.

- Adam - Man
- Seth - Appointed
- Enos - Mortal
- Cainan - Sorrow
- Mahalaleel - Blessed God
- Jared - Come Down
- Enoch - Teaching, Educated, or Dedicated
- Methuselah - His Death Shall Bring
- Lamech - Despairing, Poor, or Made Low
- Noah - Rest or Comfort

We know that Seth's line is continued through Noah, Shem, Ham, and Japheth, but what we do not know is where their wives came from. It is possible that the sons of Noah married the daughters of Cain, but that would make the flood pointless to all that hold this belief. If God's intentions were to wipe out the earth because of this mixing, that means He would have failed by only saving a group of people in mixed marriages. There is no Biblical evidence to support the theory that Seth's line could not mix with the line of Cain. It is entirely possible that Noah, Shem, Ham, and Japheth had wives that came from the line of Cain, but again, the Bible is completely silent on the issue. Genesis 4:26 also offers us an interesting insight to something else about Seth's line.

> "And to Seth, to him also there was born a son; and he called his name Enos: then began men to call upon the name of the LORD." - Genesis 4:26

Supporters of the Lines of Seth view use this verse to support the theory that Seth's line was godly because Enos began calling upon the name of the Lord. If that is true, who did Adam, Cain, Abel, and Seth call upon?

The traditional Jewish interpretation of this verse, though, implies that it marked the beginning of idolatry, i.e. that men started dubbing "Lord" things that were mere creatures. This is because the previous generations, notably Adam, had already "begun calling upon the name of the Lord", which forces us to interpret *huchal* not as "began" but as the homonym "profaned". In this light, Enos suggests the notion of a humanity (Enoshut) thinking of itself as an absolute rather than in relation to God.[1]

As we start to unravel the myth of Seth's line being righteous, we begin to see that this was not the traditional Jewish belief. Seth's son Enos is viewed as the first idolater and the rest of Seth's sons initiate disobedience to God by making wives of Cain's daughters, if we hold to that view. Are these the actions that we would expect from a godly line?

Genealogy Of Cain

Cain seems to get a bad rap for his actions, but God forgave him. Not only did God forgive him, but also He placed a mark on Cain and promised to avenge him sevenfold (Genesis 4:15) if anyone killed him. This mark does not sound like the mark of a curse, but the mark of God's blessing. It is true that Cain made a mistake, but that does not make his entire line ungodly, as some would have us believe. Cain is a perfect example of God's

---

[1] http://en.wikipedia.org/wiki/Enos_(Bible)

grace and mercy. Let's look at what the Bible says about the people in Cain's lineage.

- Cain - Possession or Spear
- Enoch - Teaching, Educated, or Dedicated
- Irad - Donkey, City of Witness, or Fugitive
- Mehujael - Struck by God
- Methusael - Man Who Asked God
- Lamech - Despairing, Poor, or Made Low
- Jubal - Ram
- *Naamah (daughter) - Pleasant
- Tubal-Cain - Worldly Possession

This is the last mention of Cain's genealogy, which becomes important in refuting the many false doctrines surrounding Cain's bloodline. Some scholars would have us believe that because Cain killed Abel, his entire line is cursed, but that simply is not true. The Bible does not make any reference to Cain's line being cursed or any commandment for them not to mix with Seth's line. For this view to hold up, one needs to add their personal opinion to the text and dismiss actual scripture. The following questions need to be answered if we are to accept the view that Cain's line was ungodly:

- Why were Seth's sons taking wives of their own choosing?
- Why were Seth's sons disobeying a command of God if they were godly?

Seth's line is the one that seems to be acting against the will of God if we actually read the story. They initiate the disobedience by taking wives of their own choosing. It seems as though the "daughters of Cain" had no say in the matter, and the sons of Cain did not participate in this event. Everyone in Cain's line seems to be completely innocent as far as the text of Genesis 6:1-4 is concerned. The facts seem to support the exact opposite of what the Lines of Seth Theory teaches. According to scripture, Cain's line seems to be neutral in these events and Seth's sons seem to initiate the defiance of God. If we hold to this particular view we are no longer relying on scripture to shape our belief, but are actually preaching our own gospel. While we are on the subject of Cain, let's explore a few other false teachings about this man of God.

Hidden Serpent Seed Doctrine

❖ Adam genetically passed on homosexuality to the rest of the human race.

❖ God is a liar and does not keep His promises.

Debunked In This Chapter

✓ Debunked: Adam was not Cain's father.

✓ Debunked: Cain does not appear in Adam's genealogy.

✓ Debunked: The mark of Cain was a curse.

✓ Debunked: Abel was older than 130 when he died.

✓ Debunked: Lamech killed Cain.

Chapter 3: The Curse of Canaan

According to Serpent Seed Theorists, Cain's line was continued through Noah's wife via Canaan. The theory states that it was Ham that snuck into Noah's tent while Noah was drunk and had sex with his own mother. Let's take a look at the verse in question.

> "And Ham, the father of Canaan, saw the nakedness of his father, and told his two brethren without." - Genesis 9:22

The first thing that we should notice is that Ham saw the nakedness of his father. Serpent Seed Theorists take this to mean that he actually had sex with his mother. Let's look at the Hebrew words used in this passage.

- Saw - raah (see, discern, become aware of)
- Nakedness - ervah (shame, nakedness, undefended parts)

As we can see, there is absolutely nothing to suggest that sex occurred between Ham and his mother. Serpent Seed Theorists usually attempt to support the twisting of the above verse by pointing out the following verse.

> "The nakedness of thy father's wife shalt thou not uncover: it is thy father's nakedness." - Leviticus 18:8

The problem with using this verse is that it specifically refers to the act of "uncovering". In Genesis 9:22 it is clear that Ham saw the nakedness of his father, but the passage makes no mention of him uncovering anyone. Serpent Seed Theorists have a tendency to play loosely with the text. The word used for "uncover" in Leviticus 18:8 is *galah*, which does not mean the same as *raah*.

Another problem we encounter is that Ham went out and told his brothers that his father was naked. If Ham actually had sex with his mother, why would he run out and tell his brothers? The most likely conclusion is that Ham did not have sex with his mother as evident by the English and the original Hebrew. When we accept the Bible at face value, the false view of this theory is easily debunked.

✓ Debunked: Ham had sex with his mother.

Was The Curse Placed On Ham or Canaan?

There is a lot of confusion among believers in general as to whether the curse was placed on Ham or Caanan. When we read the scripture, we can clearly see who the recipient of the curse was.

> "And Noah awoke from his wine, and knew what his younger son had done unto him. And he said, Cursed be Canaan; a servant of servants shall he be unto his brethren." - Genesis 9:24-25

The verse is clear that Noah (not God) cursed Canaan. The second thing we need to take note of is that it is assumed that Ham is the younger son, but when we examine scripture, we see that Ham is always mentioned in the middle. In the following passages we find Ham listed in the middle of the group:

- Genesis 5:32
- Genesis 6:10
- Genesis 7:13
- Genesis 9:18

That does not concretely prove that Ham was not the younger son, but as always, we need to look at the Hebrew words used here.

- Younger - qatan (youngest, smallest, least important)
- Son - ben (son, grandson, sons' sons)

In the light of scripture we see that the word ben can be used to refer to a grandson, great grandson, and so on. Notice that the words grandfather, grandson, uncle, aunt, etc. are never used in the Bible. The Hebrew words, along with the fact that Noah cursed Canaan, leads to the safe assumption that it was Canaan that did something to Noah that was worthy of a curse.

According to Serpent Seed Theorists, it was Ham that committed this act. If that is true, why would Noah curse Canaan and not Ham? Ham also had three other sons that were not included in the curse. One final problem we face is that Serpent Seed Theorists teach that Canaan was conceived when Ham had sex with his own mother. If that is true, why did Noah curse Canaan by name the very next morning if he had just been conceived the night before? How did he know his wife was pregnant, only several hours after having sex? Why would Ham still name his son Canaan even after the curse Noah placed on his unborn son? None of it makes sense when we take a serious look at the theory.

- ✓ Debunked: The phrase "youngest son" refers to Ham.
- ✓ Debunked: Ham was cursed.

Did Cain's Line Survive The Flood

Serpent Seed Theorists have a problem when it comes to the flood in Noah's day because according to the Bible they should have been wiped out. As usual with false doctrines, the scripture needs to be twisted, added to, or ignored altogether in order to get the theory to fit. What does the Bible say about who survived the flood?

> "And Noah went in, and his sons, and his wife, and his sons' wives with him, into the ark, because of the waters of the flood." - Genesis 7:7

> "In the selfsame day entered Noah, and Shem, and Ham, and Japheth, the sons of Noah, and Noah's wife, and the three wives of his sons with them, into the ark;" - Genesis 7:13

These verses are clear that Noah, his wife, his sons (Shem, Ham, Japheth), and their three wives were the only people to enter the ark. If we add up the number of people mentioned, there are a total of eight.

25

"And every living substance was destroyed which was upon the face of the ground, both man, and cattle, and the creeping things, and the fowl of the heaven; and they were destroyed from the earth: and Noah only remained alive, and they that were with him in the ark." - Genesis 7:23

"Which sometime were disobedient, when once the longsuffering of God waited in the days of Noah, while the ark was a preparing, wherein few, that is, eight souls were saved by water" - 1 Peter 3:20

These verses make it clear that only eight people survived the flood. No matter how much twisting is done to the scripture, it is clear that nobody snuck on the boat. Nobody went underground, or hid in the mountains. Everything was wiped out. When we take that Bible at face value and do not attempt to twist it to fit our view, we see that there is no way Cain's line could have survived the flood.

✓ Debunked: Cain's line survived the flood.

Was Noah's Wife From Cain's Line?

Because Serpent Seed Theorists face a huge problem with the flood of Noah, they need to twist scripture in order to create a way for the theory to progress past the flood. According to their belief, Noah's wife was from the line of Cain and when Ham got her pregnant, the line of Cain continued through Canaan. There are two major problems with this belief. If we read the entire genealogy in Genesis 5, we see that Noah is a descendant of Seth. In the Bible, the line is always continued through the man, which means that if Noah is from the line of Seth, so are Shem, Ham, and Japheth. Even if Noah's wife was from the line of Cain, her son with Ham would still be considered to be from Seth's line. Besides not stating what line Noah's wife was from, the Bible also states that Shem, Ham, and Japheth were all born when Noah was 500. Noah is only mentioned as having one wife, so it is impossible for one of his sons to bear offspring from the line of Cain.

We encounter a similar scenario in the book of Ruth. Ruth is a Moabitess and Boaz is from the tribe of Judah. Ruth and Boaz have a son named Obed, he then has a son named Jesse, and Jesse then has a son named David. David is from the line of Judah. Nowhere in the entire story are any of these men referred to as being a Moabite. The point is that the genealogy is not attributed to the woman, but to the man. The attempt to find a way around the flood is easily debunked when we look at scripture honestly.

Because of the above scenario that does not allow for Cain's line to survive the flood, there is another huge doctrinal leap that teaches that Noah may have had multiple wives. The reasoning is that since the Bible does not say that Noah only had one wife, they work under the assumption that he did get a woman from the line of Cain pregnant and attribute Ham as the offspring of that relationship. However, as stated above, since genealogy is passed through the man, Ham would still be considered to be from the line of Seth. Serpent Seed Theorists need to invent elements to the story in order to get around the fact that Noah had all three sons when he was 500 years old (Genesis 5:32). If they admit that Noah's three sons were triplets, their entire belief structure falls apart by Genesis 6. The twisting allows them to maintain the belief in Satan's seed surviving the flood.

✓ Debunked: Canaan was from the line of Cain.

Hidden Serpent Seed Doctrine

❖ Noah had multiple wives.
❖ The Bible is wrong about who was cursed.

Debunked In This Chapter

✓ Debunked: Ham had sex with his mother.
✓ Debunked: The phrase "youngest son" refers to Ham.
✓ Debunked: Ham was cursed.

27

✓ Debunked: Cain's line survived the flood.
✓ Debunked: Canaan was from the line of Cain.

Chapter 4: Jesus and The Pharisees

Serpent Seed Theorists try to drive their point home by using the words of Christ and John in order to construct a genealogy. Once we actually read what was going on, there are a few things we will notice. The first and most important thing we will see is that many verses are purposely ignored or avoided. In this chapter we will address some of the verses that they use to present the theory and some of the verses they seem to just overlook.

The Genealogy of The Pharisees

When we turn to John 8, we find that Jesus is having a debate with the Pharisees, in which He makes a few statements that have been taken drastically out of context. First lets look at the verse that is usually ignored when Serpent Seed Theorists make their argument.

> "I know that ye are Abraham's seed; but ye seek to kill me, because my word hath no place in you." - John 8:37

If the verse is taken in context, we see two important opposition to the Serpent Seed Theory. The first on is that Jesus acknowledges that the Pharisees are the seed of Abraham. Here is the Greek word translated as seed in this passage.

- Seed - sperma (seed, descendants)

As we can see, Jesus acknowledges that they are the seed of Abraham and not the seed of the serpent. Jesus also made reference to the Pharisees wanting to kill Him, which is vastly important when we look at the next verse that is used by Serpent Seed Theorists to support their view.

> "Ye are of your father the devil, and the lusts of your father ye will do. He was a murderer from the beginning, and abode not in the truth, because there is no truth in him. When he speaketh a lie, he speaketh of his own: for he is a liar, and the father of it." - John 8:44

29

It is the first part of this verse that is used by Serpent Seed Theorist in support of their view. However, when we look at the phrase, "ye are of your father the devil" in Greek, we find a completely different meaning than a genealogy.

- Of - ek (of, under, derived)

The word *ek* is a Greek preposition that denotes the origin of one's actions or motion. What were the actions of the Pharisees? They were trying to kill Jesus as we read in John 8:37. When we read the chapter in context, we see that Jesus actually said that the Pharisees were Abraham's descendants, but their actions come from Satan. John 8:44 is clearly not a genealogy.

✓ Debunked: The Pharisees are from the line of Cain.

The Kenite Doctrine

The more we explore these false teachings about Cain, the stranger the ideas get. One such false idea is that Cain is the father of the Kenites and as such, the Kenites are cursed. Racist groups and individuals propose the idea that the Kenites are either African or Jewish, depending on who is teaching this theory. Genesis Chapter 4 is the only scriptural reference to Cain's genealogy and the flood in Genesis Chapter 6 wipes out all of mankind except Noah's family. How is it possible that Cain fathered the Kenites if the Kenites are not mentioned until after the flood? According to the Bible, there is absolutely no truth to this belief.

The Kenites as a nation are mentioned exactly seven times in the Bible and not a single reference mentions them being the descendants of Cain. Associating them with Cain is man's doing in order to encourage racism and self-interest. When we look into the words of the Bible, we can actually trace the true origin of the Kenites.

Moses father in law Jethro was a Midianite and so was his other father in law Hobab. Hobab was referred to as "the son of Raguel the Midianite" (Numbers 10:29). In Judges 4:1 we find that Heber is of the children of Hobab, but he is referred to as a Kenite. If this is true, the Kenite line started with someone from the line of Hobab and not the line of Cain, as some would have us believe. Understanding the terminology of the time is very important when tracing genealogy. The words grandfather, grandmother, grandson, and granddaughter are never used in the Bible. Everyone is referred to as a father, mother, son, or daughter regardless of how many generations apart they are. Heber may have been Hobab's great grandson, great great grandson, or even farther in the generational line for all we know, but the Bible is 100% clear that the Kenites started with someone in the line of Hobab.

Who are The Real Jews?

There are some that believe the term "Jew" only refers to the house of Judah and that is the only tribe that are chosen of God. However, it is important to understand that the term Jew is not the same as the Hebrews, which is used to describe the descendants of Abraham. God made the promise to all of the Hebrews and not just a sub set. In modern terminology, the word Jew is used to describe the religion of the Hebrew people.

There are many groups of people that claim to be the "real" Jews and interestingly, most of these groups have a race based agenda. They also usually do not accept that God's promise to restore Israel to her land took place in 1948. Some groups claim that the Promised Land is really America and some claim Africa, but who are the real Jews according to the Bible?

"For he is not a Jew, which is one outwardly; neither is that circumcision, which is outward in the flesh: But he is a Jew, which is one inwardly; and circumcision is that of the heart, in the spirit, and not in the letter; whose praise is not of men, but of God." - Romans 2:28-29

31

Paul tells us that a real Jew is one that inwardly circumcised and seeks the praises of God. This verse echoes what Jesus was telling the Pharisees being more focused on religion than on relationship.

> "He answered and said unto them, Well hath Esaias prophesied of you hypocrites, as it is written, This people honoureth me with their lips, but their heart is far from me." – Mark 7:6

Both Jesus and Paul establish that Judaism is based on faith and has nothing to do with nationality. Serpent Seed Theorists usually neglect to mention this fact when presenting their theory. As a result, they point to verses like Revelation 3:9 and make the claim that Christ is talking about people who claim a false lineage as opposed to pretending to follow God. Although the original use of the word Jew referred directly to those from the line of Judah, language changes over time, and Paul demonstrates that the use of the word in his time no longer referred only to a specific tribe.

✓ Debunked - Jew still only refers to the tribe of Judah.

Will Satan Have Children?

There are some that believe that Satan will indeed bare at least one child at some point in human history. This belief is based on Genesis 3:15. God prophesies that there will be conflict between the seed of the woman and the seed of the serpent. The seed of the woman clearly refers to Christ, which leads many to believe that the serpent's seed refers to the Antichrist.

> "He answered and said unto them, He that soweth the good seed is the Son of man; The field is the world; the good seed are the children of the kingdom; but the tares are the children of the wicked one; The enemy that sowed them is the devil; the harvest is the end of the world; and the reapers are the angels." - Matthew 13:38

This parable is used to say that Jesus is talking about actual bloodlines and not being a believer vs. being a non-believer in Christ. However, both John and Paul make it clear who the children of God are.

> "But as many as received him, to them gave he power to become the sons of God, even to them that believe on his name:" - John 1:12

> "For as many as are led by the Spirit of God, they are the sons of God." - Romans 8:14

> For ye are all the children of God by faith in Christ Jesus. - Galatians 3:26

The Bible is clear that we are only able to become the children of God once we accept Christ. One thing that remains constant with Serpent Seed Theorists is only interpreting part of the text so that words are changed to mean what they want them to mean. If we apply the law of interpretation which states that A+B must always equal C, then we have to conclude that the "wheat" in the passage are Jesus' literal offspring as well. We reach this conclusion because the act of "sewing" is interpreted by Serpent Seed Theorists to mean sex. Yet, when asked this question, many will deny that Christ had any offspring, as a result they reveal their practice of selective interpretation.

The Fruit Of This Belief

As with many false doctrines we can tell their origin by the fruit that the doctrine bears. The Serpent Seed Theory is held mainly by those in the Christian Identity movement, which is a group closely tied to White Supremacy. There are two versions of this belief and the one presented in this book is known as the Two-Seedline (Serpent Seed). The second belief is known as One-Seedline, which states that all men came from Adam, but only the white race is God's chosen race. The first part of this theory is to convince people that there is an evil line of people that were sired by Lucifer in the garden. Once people are sucked into this, they later teach that the Jews currently in Israel are "fake Jews" and descend from the line of Cain and are thus the seed of Lucifer. The entire goal of the theory is anti-Semitic. This is the very same doctrine upon which Hitler based the Holocaust. The Jews have been hated all throughout history and this theory is just another way to mask that hatred under the guise of scripture.

Another fruit of this doctrine is the claim that if you do not accept it you are blind, deceived, scared of the truth, and a Kenite yourself. However, it seems that those that do not accept this theory are actually basing their decision on sound Biblical doctrine and not farfetched theories that twist scripture in an effort to perpetrate a false doctrine.

> "For the time will come when they will not endure sound doctrine; but after their own lusts shall they heap to themselves teachers, having itching ears; And they shall turn away their ears from the truth, and shall be turned unto fables." - 2 Timothy 4:3-4

People ultimately believe this doctrine not because it can be supported by scripture, but because they refuse to adhere to sound Biblical doctrine.

The Targum of Jonathan

The Targum Jonathan is often quoted by Serpent Seed Theorists to support their claims that Eve had sex with Satan in the garden. Before we get into this particular Targum, its important to understand exactly what a Targum is. A Targum is an Aramaic translation of the Hebrew Bible, written between the second temple period and the early middle ages. Targumim (plural) are not word for word translations, but more of a commentary that favors allegory over literalism.

There are two Targumim in question when we talk about the Targum of Jonathan. The first is attributed to Jonathan ben Uzziel and the second is referred to as Pseudo Jonathan. The Targum Jonathan is considered the official Targum of the prophets and does not contain the book of Genesis. The Targum that Serpent Seed Theorists usually refer to is Pseudo Jonathan.

The Targum of Pseudo Jonathan is a Western translation of the Torah, and the official title is the Targum of Jerusalem. This particular Targum contains Aggadic material, which consists of folklore, myth, and legend, not just scripture. The actual text itself is believed to have been composed between the 8th and 15th century.

Serpent Seed Theorists have a tendency to put the Targum of Pseudo Jonathan on the same level as scripture, but it is actually just one person's interpretation of scripture. When this Targum is quoted from, it is very important to understand that it holds no more weight than any other modern day commentaries.

A Challenge To Serpent Seed Theorists

I would like to challenge any Serpent Seed Theorists that believe that Cain being the son of Lucifer is sound Biblical doctrine, to prove their point using only a KJV and a Strong's Concordance. Sound Biblical doctrine needs to start with the Bible as the foundation of the entire theory, and once that is established, outside sources can be used to enhance the theory. However, if outside sources need to be used to add to the Bible, it is not sound Biblical doctrine.

✓ Debunked: Serpent Seed Theorists follow sound Biblical doctrine.

Hidden Serpent Seed Doctrine

- ❖ Other texts hold just as much weight as the Bible.
- ❖ The Jews in Israel are the seed of Satan.

Debunked In This Chapter

- ✓ Debunked: The Pharisees are from the line of Cain.
- ✓ Debunked: Serpent Seed Theorists follow sound Biblical doctrine.
- ✓ Debunked: Jew still only refers to the tribe of Judah.

Minister Dante Fortson was born November 15, 1982 in Las Vegas, NV, to Pastor Perryetta Lacy. As a child, growing up in his grandparents' house, Minister Dante Fortson had many experiences that have helped shape his belief in God and the supernatural. As a result of a dream one night and hearing his name being called in the house the following morning, he was saved and baptized at a very young age.

In elementary school he would read about vampires, ghosts, and other supernatural phenomena every chance he had. As he neared the 8th grade, Minister Fortson developed a sudden interest in UFOs, aliens, and the occult. One night, after a seemingly failed attempt to channel what he believed to be extra-terrestrials, a life changing demonic experience left him with a lasting fear of the dark and led him to start studying the Bible more intensely for an explanation of the events. It has been a little over a decade since Minister Fortson became a student of Bible prophecy. Now, a self-proclaimed expert in demonology, angelology, and the supernatural, he freely shares his knowledge and experience with anyone seeking advice in spiritual matters.

The road to becoming a minister was not easy for Minister Fortson. Of all of his life experiences, the one single event that led him back into his calling was going to jail December 19, 2008. After 80 days between County and City Jails, he was released, and shortly thereafter, he started his official ministry training. Just over a decade after he began intensely studying the bible, Minister Dante Fortson was licensed on July 26, 2009. Now that he has stepped into his calling, he believes that he can finally do the work he has been called to do since that day he first heard God's voice in his grandparents' house.

God's work through him is just beginning. His goal is simple and familiar. Go ye therefore and teach all nations. Through his writing he plans to do just what Jesus commissioned His disciples to do before His ascension.

Is The Rapture In The Bible?

Is the Rapture actually in the Bible or is it really a delusion made up by Margaret McDonald in 1830? What does the Bible say about escaping the coming Tribulation? Minister Dante Fortson answers these questions and many more in this 2 disc set. Your view on the Rapture will never be the same again.

Special Double Disc CD Set

20% Off When You Order Online

Top 7 Signs of
A False Teacher

There are a lot of things that have been going on behind the scenes that you as readers are not aware of. There has been constant bullying by one side and the other side has been hesitant to take action. There were several things that I've been wanted to address for a couple of months now, but at the request of certain people that I respect, I have held off. I'm not really one to be intimidated or bullied, so last week I posted notice that my prior standing agreement has expired.

Before I proceed, please understand that my problem with these individuals is not personal, but doctrinal. When Jesus confronted problems with the doctrine of the Pharisees, He did not wait for months to address it, He did not ignore it, and He did not try to set up meetings behind the scenes. He addressed it on the spot so that His silence would not be mistaken as agreement. When we delay responding to false teaching, it is my opinion that we might as well co-sign it in agreement. The longer we keep silent by false teaching, the more people there are that are ultimately affected by it. With that said, here are the signs of someone that is teaching falsely.

#1: Failure To Provide Scripture: One trend among false teachers is to mix in enough truth in order to sound reliable, but at the same time mix in other ideas that are not found in scripture. When personal opinion is mixed in, it should be made 100% clear that it is such. You have every right to ask for a scripture reference, no matter how much you trust the person doing the teaching. Acts 17:11 encourages us to do so without regard to the person we are listening to. If it is not backed by scripture, it is not scripture.

#2: Recite Tradition As Scripture: Many people believe that tradition = Biblical. However, that his not always the case. There are many traditions in the church that have no scriptural backing, but many Christians still believe they are Biblical. No matter how long a tradition has been around, it will never be Biblical if it is not supported at all.

#3: The Heresy Card: When someone can't completely back their position using only the Bible, they have a tendency to throw out the "heresy card" in order to maintain their grasp on their followers. Many people won't bother to look into something that has been branded as heresy, and as a result of this fear based leadership tactic, we end up with situations like David Koresh and Jim Jones.

Please keep in mind that the original dissenters from the Catholic Church were branded as heretics. In the end, it was the Catholic Church that were the real heretics. Because of the branding, many people were scared to go against the established Church Doctrine. Once again, traditional Church teaching does not = scripture.

#4: Refusal To Do Research: Acts 17:11 tells us to listen then research. Proverbs 18:13 tells us that anyone that makes up their mind before researching the matter is a fool. Many false teachers have made up their mind on a given topic before ever researching it. Be very cautious of anyone that has not done the research, but claims that it's not Biblical before looking at the evidence.

Question: Why would you listen to someone that hasn't done the research?

#5: Fail To Make Personal Opinions Clear: When any teacher is giving their personal opinion, it should be 100% clear that it is not scripture. My personal opinion is that it is the job of the teacher to teach and then let the listener make up their own mind.

#6: Control Freak: Many times you will find these types of teachers making lists of what kind of music you should be listening to, clothing you should wear, where you can go, what you can do in your bedroom (even as a married couple), and most importantly what you have to believe. The Bible is the only rule maker for our lives. If someone has a list of rules for you to follow, tell them to show it to you in the Bible. If they can't, its ultimately between you and God whether or not it is right or wrong for you to do.

#7: Denial of Scripture: This is perhaps the most common among false teachers. They will completely refuse to acknowledge any section of scripture that challenges their personal beliefs. You will find that they will defend an idea, such as Replacement Theology, but ignore every verse that says God will not abandon Israel.

Many times, you will find that false teachers do not want to debate publically because they are in fear of being proven wrong. Many times they will get upset if you respond with scripture that goes against what they are teaching.

Red Flag: Any teacher of the Bible that is offended by scripture should be avoided at all costs.

What To Do If You Discover False Teaching

I guess this would depend on whether you are a teacher yourself or a student. If you address the situation and the person acknowledges your correction, it was probably just an honest mistake or a difference in interpretation. I wouldn't classify this person as a false teacher.

If you run into a scenario like the above, following them is perfectly fine. None of us are perfect or have all of the answers. However, if you run into a teacher that is clearly not teaching from the Bible, you should stop following them immediately. Sometimes we have a problem admitting when we have been deceived because we would all like to think that we are above being led astray. The only shame in being misled is failure to acknowledge and correct the situation.

Stay tuned as there are more articles to come as I address some of the false teaching that has been floating around lately. Let's see if we can get a scriptural response from some of these people in question.

Is Your Church Ignoring The Elephant In The Room?

The longer I'm in the ministry of the supernatural, the more people tell me that their church won't touch the subject of UFOs and alien abduction. All over the world people are experiencing something that they can't quite explain. Where are people supposed to turn when they can't discuss the strange lights in the sky with their pastor? The only place they can turn is to the secular world that is all too ready to preach the Alien Gospel to them.

If your pastor is scared of the subject or doesn't know where to start, I encourage you to direct him or her to this post. The subject of UFOs and Alien abduction is directly related to Biblical events. As Christians we believe we have an enemy known as Satan. However, he has many fallen angels and demons at his disposal, and their goal is deception. If you want to stop a tree from growing, you don't start cutting at the top and go down, you destroy the root so it cannot grow. So what is the root of the UFO deception?

The deception that is digging at the roots of the church is the Sethite View of Genesis 6. The theory teaches that the sons of God = The sons of Seth and The daughters of men = the daughters of Cain. However, the words Seth and Cain do not appear anywhere in the Genesis 6. The most disturbing view in the church's opinion is the alternate interpretation. Angels came down and had sex with human women in order to produce hybrid offspring.

If the pastor doesn't believe it is possible for angels to have sex, then the enemy has successfully dug up the root of his problem. UFOs and Alien abductions have nothing to do with little green or grey men from space. It has everything to do with what was going on in Genesis 6.

> "But as the days of Noah were, so shall also the coming of the Son of man be. For as in the days that were before the flood they were eating and drinking, marrying and giving in marriage, until the day that Noe entered into the ark, And knew not until the flood came, and took them all away; so shall also the coming of the Son of man be." – Matthew 24:37-39

Genesis 6 is only part of the Noah story, but again we encounter a common deception. It is commonly taught that the world will be going on as usual and get caught off guard. If we look at who was marrying in the days of Noah, we find that the only reference is to the sons of God marrying the daughters of men. Notice that Jesus uses the word "they", which does not seem to be an accident.

> "And whereas thou sawest iron mixed with miry clay, they shall mingle themselves with the seed of men: but they shall not cleave one to another, even as iron is not mixed with clay." – Daniel 2:43

Notice that Daniel uses the same word "they". It is a personal pronoun, which means in the context of Daniel, "they" are something other than the seed of men. Both Jesus and Daniel make a reference to "they" in context to the last days. Jesus references the days of Noah and Daniel references a strange mixing. If we use Jesus and Daniel as our blueprint we can explain both UFOs and Alien abductions. If the sons of God are indeed angels, Genesis 6 has the following in common with alien abduction:

- Strange beings abduct women of their choosing.
- Sex occurs.
- Hybrids are created.

For those of you reading this for the first time, the hybrids I'm referring to are the Nephilim. Googling the word will give you enough information to figure out exactly what the Hebrews believed the Nephilim to be. For those that don't believe angels can have sex based on Matthew 22:30, please understand that Lucifer's angels are NOT angels of God and they are NOT in heaven. That means the rules about marriage no longer apply to them. Also notice that is says "do not", but it does not say that they are incapable of marrying or performing a sexual act.

Finally, let's look at something else that puts UFOs and Alien abduction in context. Over and over again, people have reported that these "alien" beings have told them that Jesus is just an alien or an ascended master, but not the son of God. Why are they so concerned with Jesus? Paul seemed to have an insight that can only really be understood within the context of alien abduction:

> "But though we, or an angel from heaven, preach any other gospel unto you than that which we have preached unto you, let him be accursed." - Galatians 1:8

Is this just a general statement or is it a warning? Why would an angel preach another Gospel? Paul also makes another statement that adds a little bit of clarity to his previous words.

> "Now the Spirit speaketh expressly, that in the latter times some shall depart from the faith, giving heed to seducing spirits, and doctrines of devils;" - 1 Timothy 4:1

Why would people depart from the faith and listen to demons and seducing spirits? What kind of event would cause this falling away? If fallen angels showed up and claimed to be fallen angels, very few people would denounce God to follow them. However, if they showed up and PRETENDED to be extraterrestrials, then people have tangible "creators" to believe in, thus negating the need to believe in God, Christ, and the supernatural altogether.

> "Let no man deceive you by any means: for that day shall not come, except there come a falling away first, and that man of sin be revealed, the son of perdition; Who opposeth and exalteth himself above all that is called God, or that is worshipped; so that he as God sitteth in the temple of God, shewing himself that he is God." – 2 Thessalonians 2:3-4

And the next verse:

> "And for this cause God shall send them strong delusion, that they should believe a lie: That they all might be damned who believed not the truth, but had pleasure in unrighteousness." – 2 Thessalonians 2:11-12

There are a couple of things to note in 2 Thessalonians which will be important to all Christians. Notice the falling away (apostasy) has to come first. That means Christians will still be here when this deception takes place. That opens the doors for the Antichrist to come later. Again, is your church ignoring the elephant in the room? Pastors, are you leaving your flock unarmed and open to one of the greatest deceptions the world has ever seen?

> "**My people are destroyed for lack of knowledge**: because thou hast rejected knowledge, I will also reject thee, that thou shalt be no priest to me: seeing thou hast forgotten the law of thy God, I will also forget thy children." – Hosea 4:6

Pastors, don't let your people be destroyed because they lack knowledge. The job of the church is not to avoid things because we do not understand them. We are to educate and empower the flock so that they will not be caught off guard. If you are a pastor that doesn't know how to approach this subject or you don't know where to start, my new book is 328 pages of information on this subject. If you are a Christian that has questions and don't know where to turn, I encourage you to start at the root and learn the truth about Genesis 6.

27193639R00032

Made in the USA
Lexington, KY
31 October 2013